THE HOURGLASS

ISHITA AKOLKAR

Made with ❤ on the Notion Press Platform
www.notionpress.com

To my dad, my family,
and to friendships everywhere.

Contents

Contents

Contents

Contents

Foreword

The Hourglass is Ishita's second volume of her poems after The Unscrambled Heart. In 'The Hourglass' she has beautifully woven her thoughts and imagination which enroute us to a dreamy world. We are amazed to see her growth from a humble child to a notable poetess. Proud to have been a tiny part of her successful poetic journey. The Hourglass is a must-read collection.

- Naveen Vadial,

Academician

The write-up is extraordinary. As I was reading, I felt as if it was written about my life events. I had horripilation when I was reading the end part. Once a more important part of our life, a friend, who is your family, a sibling, an enemy, there is no proper word to describe that relation, vanishes somewhere, you keep memorizing the quality time spent and never realize days turning into months and years and years pass by. You almost brought tears to my eyes. I miss my friends so badly. My heart is whimpering and longing to meet them. We have seen each other crying, happy, disturbed, fighting, and whatnot. It was just us, no families around and today we are so entangled in our own families that all that are now memories. I am surely gonna send a few of the pages to my friends from your book once it's printed.

-Dr. Gulshan Avadia Ayachit,

Consultant Physiotherapist, MPT (SPORTS)

Preface

'The Hourglass' is a story of an everyday friendship. The story of how a stranger can enter your life, brighten it, make you cry, make you laugh, and slowly turn back into a stranger again. This book is an ode to friendship.

It's the story of how two people meet, fight, reconcile, grow, and miss each other years along the way. The book is divided into the aforesaid five chapters.

The first chapter 'We Met' contains 10 poems. This number of poems signifies that when you first grow friends with someone, you're excited to be with them and slowly learn about them.

The next chapter, 'We Fought' contains 20 poems. The first big fight in a friendship is a crucial stage. There's so much going on. You want to say so much to each other; this chapter is all about it.

The third chapter 'We Reconciled' contains 15 poems. It's the number between the first two chapters, signifying that after you patch up you're closer than you initially were but there's a knot on the thread now. This shows that however close you get, there would be some differences between you.

The fourth chapter 'We Grew' has 21 poems. This is the time

when you move from your teenage phase to a path where you start leading your career-driven lives. The chapter is all about what you go through when you're growing up, which is a lot; hence, most poems are in this chapter.

The last chapter, 'We Missed' has 14 poems. This chapter is about when you're comparatively older, successful, and independent. This is when you start missing your friends. It's about the age where you have moved on from one another but can't move on from the younger years you had with them.

There are too many books about romantic heartbreak, but not enough about the heartbreak that you go through when you lose a friend. This book is for all those friendships.

Author's Note

Friendships, they're such an essential part of our lives. They're the family that *we* choose for ourselves. They stand with us in happiness, in rain, at parties, and in pain.

Having good friends really changes everything. It changes how you work, how you think, and most importantly, how comfortable you feel about yourself.

Now, I won't pretend that I've got friends that grew up and started their own families and stuff, but I do have lost friends along the way. Maybe just because of a school change or their change of residence or just something else. But yes, I have lost friends and I often think about them in solitary.

So, this book is an ode to all the friendships I've ever had, an ode to all the friends I've lost, and an ode to the friendships I've witnessed.

To all my friends, I adore you. To all the readers, thank you for choosing this book and being my friend.

Thank you to my beta readers, you guys are the best. Thank you to my parents, my family, and my friends for the immense support I receive every day from you all. I'm so grateful for every single one of you.

Thank you.

We Met

1. Canvases of building friendships

My knee was scraped
from my first bicycle ride.
The next day I went to school
holding behind the fear
of being teased for it.
So when you asked about it,
I hated you at that moment
until you rolled up your sleeve
and showed me
how you've had got
your elbow scratched
the very same way.
Maybe the scratches
were the canvases
for building friendships.

2. Nervous

And I was nervous,
my heartbeats running faster
than they ever had.
My mind thinking
million thoughts per minute
and it all just
simply vanished
the second you stood beside me,
held my hand
and smiled.

3. Boring?

So, there I was again;
the boring place called school
where I knew everyone
yet no one seemed to know me.
I sat alone, again,
on the lonely bench
that everyone seemed to dislike
so I made it my favorite.
I brought a bag of courage
along with me
to go through the day.
But little did I know
that I wouldn't need it again,
for then you came in
with your cheery smile
and shy eyes.
You asked if you could
sit right by me
and I nodded oh so happily!
So that day,
I went home and started thinking,
'maybe school isn't

so boring after all.'

4. Sibling

I never liked you
for your brains,
neither your beauty
nor your grades.
I liked you for your heart
that inspired me
to be a better person every day.
I liked you because
when everyone smiled at me
you had the guts
to tell me when I was wrong.
I liked you because
in the world of 'besties'
you became my sibling.

5. How could we not be friends?

It's funny,
remembering the first day we met
we were so out of place;
new places
new faces
old hands blurred out.
Would we still
be so close
without that book we first talked about?
it's funny,
for now, I see us and
could never think–
for even one moment
that we would not be friends.

6. Free Verse

You told me
You were poetry,
When I told you
That I loved them,
But you never mentioned
That you didn't rhyme.
And I, with my limited
Knowledge and ideas
Thought you weren't ideal
When you were quite
The opposite.
You were a free verse
In a world
Who was trapped
Within the ideals
Of perfect lines
And pretty rhymes.
You were free
But I was stuck with
The rhymes
That left meaning
In order to match.

7. "Wanna be friends?"

And there we met-
amongst the bunch of unknown people.
Everyone new,
everyone unknown.
You knew everyone,
you always had that capacity.
You smiled
and you laughed
and everyone was charmed.
I couldn't be so-
I tried so hard,
I still do.
But then you called my name
"Hey, wanna be friends?"
and then everything-
everything just changed.

8. Friend for life

*The road was empty-
just as usual
after we left school.
I was riding on my cycle,
with the metal basket
and the too-tight pedal
and you drove beside me.
"Hey!" you said.
You had that new cycle
everyone wished they had-
The one with shiny colors
and the smoothest pedals.
You could've driven faster-
you could,
but you slowed down for me
and I knew
I had found a friend for life.*

9. "Great Friends"

"I am scared,"
I whispered to my mom.
Was it just me
who was worried about this?
I can make friends.
I can, right?
"You'll make great friends,"
she whispered back.
After the first day at school,
I knew my mom was right.

10. The friend of dreams

It's funny, right?
how you were an introvert-
the shy one of the group,
but you were the
who was the first one to talk?
You talked and talked,
I did too,
but you talked
you didn't just wait
for your turn to speak
and that was when I knew
that I had found
the friend of my dreams.

We fought

11. "Shut up"

"Shut up" I screamed,
you made me angry,
so angry.
But never in a million years
did I think how it'd be
if you actually stopped talking to me.
Who would ask me
the most random questions
about my favorite emojis of the day?
Who would get me an ice-cream
when I have a bad day?
So please,
never shut up.
For I might not say it every day
but your presence
automatically makes my life better.

12. Chance to be your friend again

Isn't it funny,
had we never met
all those years ago
then I wouldn't have to
face any pain today,
but even after all that
I would be willing to take the pain
if it meant that
I would have the chance
to be your friend again?

13. Private diary

"Please stop me."
I cried, as I wrote
another message to your name.
I couldn't stop.
My fingers had a mind
of their own
and whenever my mind
thought of you,
those fingers
etched towards your name
written in my text box.
I didn't know what else to do.
The text bar under your name
had become a private diary for me.
The diary where I shared
each moment
each idea
each fascination.
It was the sacred haven
where I spilled every single
childish thought of mine.
So when you stopped responding,

when the castle
that I had mightly boasted
crumbled overnight,
I didn't know how to recover
for with the support
of a safe heaven on earth,
I forgot
how to live
amidst the mortals.

14. Leftover batter

I made cookies today,
just like we always did.
The bowl stayed on the counter,
the leftover batter still in it
and the fingers to steal it
from right in front of me
were missing.

15. Just a joke

"it was just a joke"
I know.
I understand.
I'm sorry.
But please listen to me once,
I can't laugh at this.
I can't laugh at the normal joke
because this is what
I see myself crying
at 2 AM every night.
Because I scream at myself
trying to improve
the very same thing.
Because it was never funny
in the very first place.
"Oh god, you think too much."
I know.
I'm sorry.

16. "You don't"

"I hate you"
I screamed
at the top of my lungs.
You didn't scream back.
You sighed and with a
shake of your head,
And smiled.
"What?"
I asked still filled with anger.
"You don't," you replied
still with that
damn annoying beautiful smile,
"You could never."
I let out a breath
I never knew I was holding
and I smiled,
how could I not?
When you're standing there
with that charming smile of yours
knowing me better
than I could ever.
"No, I don't," I replied.

17. New memories

It wasn't sad when we fought,
for we fight a lot
and that is love,
but it became sad
when our stories
became memories of the past
but the new memories
were never formed.

18. Please miss me too

Sometimes, late nights,
I remember you.
Your poorly constructed jokes,
your lopsided crooked smile.
The smile that made
everyone around you laugh.
Oh, how you loved
to make everyone laugh!
And all those wandering thoughts
led me to only one conclusion
that maybe I miss you too much.
But I have a coward heart
to call you first,
So here I'm telling you:
please miss me too,
and maybe you'd have
the courage that I always had admired
to call me maybe.

19. Speaking back to the winds

The winds hound
louder than they ever had,
and I stand there
barefoot on the barren land.
The winds blow by me,
caressing my cheek,
flowing my hair.
the familiarity of it all
isn't lost in the translation.
The accolades sprinkle
right out of my mouth,
and I am having a fight;
a fight between my mind
and my mouth.
How do I perceive
the winds' talk
as someone other than you?
and moreover,
how do I stop
speaking back to it?

20. Take my heart

You take my heart;
an entity of me
comprised of my happiness
my sadness
my ideas and my thoughts.
You take it out of me.
You laugh, so brave
for doing
what everyone else
never dreamt of.
Who's gonna tell you?
or moreover
Who's gonna tell me?
you didn't just take my heart
you ripped it out
flesh and bones
bathing in blood
and I stood there
couldn't do anything.
I stood there
and let you.
I cried

I shrieked
but no one heard me
so I wrote.
I wrote until my hands
were roughed up
and they started bleeding.
I wrote until
the hollow space
in my chest
bled on the paper.
I wrote and wrote
and wrote so much.
But no one cared enough
to read.

21. The dress I wore at the last party

Today morning
I wore the dress
that I wore for that last party
we attended together.
My mascara smudge
still on the collar,
the scent of my perfume
still lingering over it.
The spaghetti that I loved that night
still stains its sauce
on the side of the dress.
And here I am,
the same person
wearing the same clothing.
So why,
this time that I wear this
I don't look the same?
Why without your
loud cheering
I don't feel the same anymore?

22. Peaceful chaos

So you just laughed
around the ineffable silence
the whisperings of the night
an impenetrable force
withstanding upon your mind.
And you laughed.
I wish I could too,
in this realm of chaos
I wish I could laugh
deep into the oblivion-
maybe the only place
where the chaos would seem
peaceful.

23. Heartbroken

So I cried
like a normal heartbroken teenager
at 3 AM.
But there's this thing
I wasn't heartbroken,
not in that sense at least.
I would prefer that over this,
"Precisely sweetheart
cause you haven't had your
heartbroken yet" they'd say.
I have.
I was on a boat
all alone in the sea
and the raft
fell
deep below the surfaces.
I had been heartbroken.

24. Unspoken speeches

I want to say something,
scratch that
I want to shout
about a lot.
I have reels of
unspoken speeches
residing inside me;
patiently waiting
to be spoken out
to someone other
than the chaotic silence
at 3 AM.

25. Don't hate us

Hate me
as much as you can
but please,
please don't hate
all that we used to have.
Please don't
have the courage
to insult
all our pretty smiles.
Don't have the courage
to insult our memories.
Don't have the courage
to hate us.

26. Hiding from you

You stole away
all my toys
from the playground
and kept pretending
that you didn't.
After years and years
of being together
I wish I'd have known
that you would take away
every ounce of happiness
poured in my bowl
and make it yours.
Why didn't I
try to hide it from you?
Why didn't I
start hiding from you?

27. Never knew you

I've seen monsters
hiding behind the veil,
I've seen angels
hiding behind the mask.
But one look at you
and I forgot
that I had also seen
the devil hiding behind
the face of human.
Maybe I never knew you
at all.

28. Drown

I drown and drown
in depths too deep
your hand over my head
Pushing me down in.
I scream and scream
in loud silence
and you leave me drowning
without another glance.
Even in the cold water
fishes don't forget
their will to live
or to stay away from the net.
My thoughts didn't drown
even when I did
my word carried on
breaking through the lid.

29. Inferior

You laughed at me
every time
I thrived.
You called it losing,
from the most superior.
You told me
that when I came second,
I was still
inferior to the first.
You laughed at me,
and shouted to the world
about how idiotic I was.
And I heard you,
I did.
But it didn't scramble me.
It couldn't.
For I knew
by the claps
of other thousands of
my well-wishers
that no matter
how inferior I was

to the person who came first,
I would always be
higher than you
who laughed at me
from the benches.

30. Pickle jar

It was a glass jar
filled with pickle in it.
And I, with my
broken fingers
and torn hands
slipped the jar
down to the ground.
And it broke
into pieces
and pieces
and pieces.
I didn't see the glass
shredding into pieces,
I saw myself
and how broken I was.
It was not my fault.
It was of the one
who let me Slip through.

We Reconciled

31. Flowing blood

We went through this,
didn't we?
We fought,
we learned,
we resolved.
We went through all that.
Then pray tell,
Hiraeth,
why am I
scraping over
old wounds
just to see proof
for my flowing blood?

32. My garden

You visited my garden.
You loved it,
exactly the way it was.
You loved the way
the waterfall caressed
the back of the leaves.
You loved the way
the flowers hugged around
the front porch
and the colors
brightened up my smiles.
You loved the way
the sparrows would visit
each dawn to meet the buds.
You said you loved it, didn't you?
But then you started
giving suggestions.
"Maybe the flowers would better
with a black vase
instead of a white one."
I thought it would,
so I changed it.

"Okay and um, maybe
the waterfall would be amazing
if changed the position of it."
That sounded fair enough too,
so I did that.
And I went home
happily
thinking I finally made
such an amazing garden
that people love!
The next day
I stepped into my porch
and saw it was painted yellow.
"Hey I thought this looked better"
and I smiled,
you put in so much work for that.
Today, I lay here
in the grass that you
replaced my waterfall with,
I'm taking care of a garden
that isn't even mine anymore.
It's who you wish
I was.

33. Saved me

I never liked attention,
couldn't bear with it.
So you were always there
to help me with it.
You never told me you were helping;
I just knew.
How you'd crack a joke
right before my presentation
or how you'd deliberately
say the wrong answer
just so I'd have the guts to tell mine.
I was the older one
but you saved me
every time.

34. Understanding

Please gauge out my eyes,
add carvings
over my heart
and paint flowers
inside my head.
Please
stop the thinking,
stop the tears
and stop me
to break the strings
attached from my heart
because even though
I understand I had to cut it out
to save myself,
I still cry
for cutting it off.
-understanding does not mean it doesn't hurt.

35. Autumn

It was autumn.
The season of
falling leaves and turtle neck tees.
The old me was waving
far ashore from the
summer beaches.
I was wilting,
just like the leaves.
And I kept thinking,
"Hey, you're changing
maybe even too much."
What I failed
to understand
was that
change didn't mean
it was always bad.
Spring will
always be back.

36. Drown with your pain

And you laugh so loud
the footsteps stop.
But oh how unaware they are
of the bleeding heart
that you keep
cleaning each minute.
Oh how unaware they are
how shattered you are
on the beneath!
The shrill silence
that you bear in your mind
upon the whisperings
of the name,
how unaware they are of that!
So they smile;
they rejoice upon a glimpse
of how strong you are.
Only if-
just if they had an idea
how much sorrow you bear
underneath that prickly skin
they'd drown with your pain.

37. Stole my umbrella

Pour out the melodies,
paint fire to the castles
and spill out the oceans,
for I cannot render
the reason
why you had to carve out my heart
and call it architecture.
I cannot fathom
how you could
plaster a flower to your scratches
and leave me
out on the pavement
bleeding-
alone.
I cannot understand
how you did all that
and I stood up
by your side
even when you stole away
my umbrella in the rain.

38. Enough

I stood there
crying on the
pavement of the lonesome street.
You walk up to me,
gently take out your napkin
and rub my tears.
I sigh,
painfully pleased by the gentleness
that I was rewarded with
for my ache.
You look at me
and start to walk away
just as another set of tears
race down again.
So I cut off my sleeve,
cleanse my tears with it,
for now, I know
no one else should do that for me.
I had me,
and that was enough.

39. Fire of hope

I was wrapped in a
blanket of darkness
with my eyes shut,
the white walls
radiated no light
and the silence
was too loud
for me to bear
just as the last leaf
was about to fall
the spark of your voice
came in my view
and burnt the fire
of hope in me.

40. "It's Okay"

I want to stop
thinking for a while.
There's a million voices
screaming inside me
waiting to be spoken out.
Kicking and breaking
each other apart.
Each voice trying to push
all the others down.
Every apology is shit,
they're all giving reasons
to how this broke me.
Each voice- a part of the
shredded glass I have rippled into,
millions of pieces,
fighting in me,
and yet,
I end up saying,
"It's okay."

41. Selfish

I was selfish.
Selfish all along.
I didn't want you
to be safe
just for yourself,
I wanted so
because only you
had the power
to save me
from myself.
And I could not,
at no cost,
lose that.
So, sorry.
I was selfish
for wanting you to
keep yourself safe.

42. Raging fire

Engulfed in the water
I jumped and jumped,
trying to get to the surface.
but was there an end?
The surface was never there
and the water kept
pulling me down.
So I stopped,
pushing up.
And I opened my eyes
to find I was breathing
in the water,
which wasn't drowning me
rather it was saving
me from the raging fire.

43. Bubble

I was trapped in a box
with keys in my hand.
In a bubble, treading lightly
so as not to burst it.
For maybe, I was happy
staying behind the walls,
where the light couldn't
trouble my eyes.

44. Crossroads

What do I do,
when I stand again
on these crossroads;
alone-as usual?
Do I wait-
wait for the winds
to hound me from behind
and push me into a road
like it does with the sea
or do I voyage my way
like a sailor would do?
Do I smile
and select the first path
that my heart chooses
or do I contemplate
every single point
that my brain conjures up?
Tell me-
Please tell me
what to do
for I no longer
am brave enough

to move from these crossroads.

45. Forgiveness

Forgiveness isn't easy-
it wasn't for me at least.
I couldn't trust easily,
you knew that
and you went on
to break my heart like that.
What do I do now?
I am a desert waiting for the rain
but you are the rainstorm
I'm scared of.

We Grew

46. Worse

You shook your head at me
when I told you
that many others
had it worse.
You shook your head in disbelief.
I couldn't understand it,
until you spoke,
"This is pathetic,
isn't it?"
I still couldn't grasp
what you were trying to say,
your ideas were always so foreign
to understand for me.
I guess you knew that
so you continued,
"You don't get it, do you?
No one does.
That's how they've
taught us to think.
Just because they have it worse
doesn't mean what you're facing
is completely invalidated.

Drowning in an ocean
or in a pool,
it's still drowning at the end."
And then I felt it,
too much.
All at once.
Maybe because that was true
but I never thought that way
for whenever I cried
they were quick
to remind me,
how others always had it worse.
And with those simple words
you broke the barricade of tears
that I had always kept up.

47. I won't fix you

Oh how many tears
did you hide
behind that gorgeous smile?
How many heartbreaks
did you suffer alone
cause you were worried
that you'd bother someone
if you let those drops out.
How much did you give out
without any expectations
of receiving anything back?
Too much.
Just too much.
So, shed a tear with me
and I'll sit with you
in a dark room
where you let out
all your worries
and I let out mine.
Cry a river with me
and I won't try
to fix you,

cause beautiful things
look pretty even when broken.
I won't fix you
cause you have the power
to heal yourself.
Just don't,
for my sake,
invalidate yourself.
For you matter so much
on this earth.

48. Applause

That day I cried,
when you told me
that you were proud
of the woman I was becoming.
I cried happy tears
for no one
seemed to remember
that encouragement
on the journey
was much more important
than the applauds
on reaching the destination.

49. Oasis

And it hurts,
oh hell, it hurts bad.
Like you've gone out
in a desert for hours
and the Oasis
is nothing but a dream.
So what do you do?
Do you stop walking
do you walk until you find a pit of water?
Tell me,
please tell me,
what do you do?
Cause here I am
just alongside you
in the oasis
crumbling beside you
shifting into sand.

50. Hushed laughter

So I stood there
on the broken stone pavement,
watching the lights
dim into darkness.
My ears
muffled in a blanket
of loud honking
and hushed laughter.

51. Dear younger me

She comes in
with the brightest smile
and the most cheerful laugh.
It's contagious,
you can't help
but just laugh back.
She has all these dreams
of what she'd be;
what she'd do
and what she'd have.
Her thoughts
they don't seem to stop.
She asks and asks
and answers them too.
She pours in the room
like a perfume
in a museum.
But then she grows up
from her phase of
barbies
and dolls
and everything pink.

ISHITA AKOLKAR

She grows up
ending up to be me.

52. 'Perfect'

And sometimes I feel
like I'm constantly
disappointing everyone.
I try,
I do, too much.
But it's never enough.
And I don't know
what more i can do.
So here I store myself;
the real me
the one who's absolutely
not perfect at all.
I keep her here,
stored in a page
from my notes app.
The perfect person
will be the one
seen by people now.

53. You talk a lot!

"Did I talk too much?",
I ask again.
And again.
Again.
In the morning,
after the late-night talk.
In the afternoon,
after the morning breakfast.
In the evening,
after the long presentation.
At midnight again,
"Did I talk too much?"
And then,
I ask again.
For I talk once
and you scrape off my heart
"You talk too much, don't you?"
I tell you about my day,
I tell you about my past
and I tell you about my goals.
You don't.
You never tell me anything.

THE HOURGLASS

I'm scared of the silence
so I talk.
And I ask you again,
"did I talk too much?"
for my heart can bear the pain
of you saying yes,
of you telling me to be quiet
(I'm familiar with it now)
but I can't
bear the fear of silence.

54. The emerging plant

They stepped
over and over
on the ground
and the plant
that was trying to emerge
got trapped in and died.

55. True colors

56. We grew

And the smiles
got masked over
by the frown lines
and the laughter
turned to a Mirage.
The time had passed
and I,
with my dainty knowledge
couldn't understand
when it did.

57. It hurts

It hurts,
doesn't it?
When you think
that on becoming
the perfect person
that you always
had wanted to be,
happiness would come
running towards you
like an old friend
meeting after years
in a flower meadow,
but it doesn't,
the beat drop
mever occurs.
Being the perfect person
doesn't matter anymore
and you don't have
any other ways
to gain the happiness.
It hurts, too much.

58. Sunlight

The sun was up,
but the light that I
longed for too long
never reached me.
But it was because of me,
for I had closed all the windows
and kept wishing
for the sunlight.

59. Save me from myself

I never feared
the horses
the knights
nor the crooked.
What I feared
was always myself,
for I had many
who would save me
from the materialistic world
but who had the courage
to save me from myself?

60. Feelings

Feelings.
What terrible things
they are!
Sometimes they make
me feel like
I'm on top of the world
even when I'm drowning in
a two feet deep pool.
Sometimes
they make me feel like
thrashing every object
in my rear view
when I'm surrounded by
happiness written on faces.
Sometimes
they make me feel like
sitting in front of the ocean
and think about absolutely nothing
when I'm there
on the dance floor.
They're just terrible,
feelings.

61. Rejoice of Independence

And I'm walking out
of the door today,
leaving behind my childhood.
So why would
those drops won't stop
flowing from my eyes?
maybe perhaps it's because
I am going in the world
where even the roses
come in with thorns
when I was perfectly happy
in my made up world
where I was
softly wrapped in a blanket
sitting in sunlight.
Maybe perhaps,
it was the grave to my childhood
or maybe it was
the rejoice of my independence.

62. Last day at my school

And today is the last day,
I get to be a student
in a school
where I've grown
for the past seven years.
Today is the last day
that I wear that uniform
that I've resented for so long.
Today is the last day
when I get to
see all those smiles together
wrapped in the charming youth.
Today is the last day,
when I am just me
and you are just you
under the shadows of the trees
that we saw growing up
since it was merely a plant.
The mosaics of the years
rolling through the reels
of my mind
and I cant focus

for today is the last day
I would stand there
as a 'student'.

63. Mine

*Oh how much have I
always resented that uniform?
Those shoes,
the braids,
the i-cards,
or even the bag?
I spent too long
resenting it
that now that I
finally am getting rid of it
I can't.
I can't.
I can't lose them
for however much I hated them,
they were all mine
at the end of the day.
So how do I explain
this stupid notion
to my friends
who assume I'm the happiest
when I'm finally free
of all those things?*

64. Illusion

They starved me for days
and then put my favourite cake
on the table in front of me.
And as the sea
runs back and forth
just to kiss the sand on the beach,
I sprinted forward
just to find out
that the cake was merely an illusion.
It was the dream
that I had dreamt for years
only to find out
that it was merely an illusion.
The world burned around me
and I ached for the warmth
because I was sleeping
in a temperature opposed to it
so I forgot what kept me safe
just to learn how to feel the warmth.

65. The story of a butterfly

I told my mom
'I might cry,
the next time
someone calls me different."
She gave me a sweet smile
and told me the story
of a little butterfly.
"When the butterfly
had emerged from its cocoon,
all the caterpillars had laughed
at how different it became.
They didn't tell her
that she was evolved.
They told her,
she was not like them.
Different is sometimes
a way that others tell you
that maybe you are better
than the ordinary."
And so,
the next time
my friends teased me

for always thinking so deeply
and being 'different',
I gave them a smile
and said 'Thank you'.
Miraculously, it was
the last time
they called me 'different'.
For now, I was
no longer ashamed
in being 'different'
so all they did was compliment me.

66. I was all I needed

But I wasn't
just the same anymore.
They ripped my poetries
and burned my books.
They flushed my inks
and threw my leads.
But even after all that
they could never
break me.
For I did not become
an artist,
with my pens and pencils
or with my books and poetries.
those leads and inks
drew drawings on paper
with my hand
and created poetries.
How could they break me,
by breaking those things?
For I was all I needed.

We Missed

67. The story of two good friends

Hey, listen,
today on the subway
a little girl asked me
"Can you tell me a story
Of two good friends?"
I smiled, how could I not?
All I remembered at that moment
was us.
Two crazy friends
who were partners
in legal crimes,
in harmless pranks
and those unfiltered laughs.
So I told her
the story of those two friends
who were known by none
yet by everyone.
The friends who were
brutally honest in joyousness
and crazily filled with kindness,

are now just a part of the crowd.
No, I couldn't tell her the last bit.
Maybe the town had to see
yet another pair of such friends
and who was I to stop
giving her a chance at it?

68. Worse than enemies

"Are you enemies now?"
asked the little girl,
as if reading thoughts
out of my mind.
"No," I replied with a sad smile.
For- let's be honest,
we are not.
I wish we were, though.
"Then?" She asked again,
Determined to know the complete story,
I took a deep breath.
"Are you still friends then?"
Her questions didn't stop,
and so I had to let out
what I had never said out loud.
"No," I said back with a soft sigh,
"We aren't friends,
but we aren't enemies too."
She looked confused,
never looking out from my face
as if trying to read it.
"That's a good thing, right?"

I shook my head, "It is worse."
"Why?"
Gosh, how hard it was to tell her
that at least
enemies had some relation between them.
The relationship of hatred,
the relation of envy
or greed or any of the sins.
But no, I could never hate you,
I hope you don't too.
"Strangers," I replied,
"We are strangers now.
And I hope you never know
how it is worse than being enemies."

69. Do you remember?

Do you still remember,
the extravagant handshake
that we created
especially for the two of us?
Do you still remember,
when we laughed for days
about the terrible joke
that we didn't remember
and still, we were laughing
because we were
too embarrassed to tell the other?
Or the pranks
that we were too scared
to follow through?
Do you still remember,
the time when
we had all the time in the world
but we decided to
play in the park
rather than watching TV?
Do you remember
when you were you

and I was still me?
Cause I do
and I may be arrogant enough
to not call you first
but I'm still the same person
in my heart
who misses you
when I see two friends together.

70. The time cycle

Echoed through my brain
were the laughs
we used to have.
And the
mosaic film reels
of my dreams
projected just your face
each night.
So I never knew
that we hadn't talked
for the past four years.
I didn't understand
that the time passed.
I just used to
wait for the day to end
to meet you in my dreams
and this cycle
flowed for years
yet I was unknown.

71. Maturity

It's been a while
since I've seen you first
still the glimmer in my eyes
upon seeing you
didn't fade
and neither did the smile
that casts upon your lips
hide behind the maturity
that we've grown in together.

72. Unrecognized

You kept track
of all my allergies.
You laughed when I told you
I couldn't eat ketchup.
But when the girl,
whom we both despised,
joined in on with you
you never looked scarier.
I remember all of your
bad habits that you tried to lose,
your side eyed glances,
your bad posture
all of it.
Today I don't even recognise
the smile that plays
on your lips.
It hurts, doesn't it?

73. Forever

"And I promise you,"
I whispered,
as we held hands
tangled by our little fingers,
"To be friends forever."
"Forever," you emphasized.
Why doesn't it
get to be that way?
Why didn't we get
the forever we promised?
cause I still tell
stories of our friendship
to strangers on the bus,
and when they ask
"Are you two still friends?"
I smile and nod,
for I don't know
how to pronounce
"No, I wouldn't even recognize
that person, with whom
I promised a friendship of eternity,
standing in front of me."

*So I just nod
and look them looking at me
with a knowing smile,
that makes me wonder
if they know how it is.
Maybe 'forever'
was never to be promised,
for had I promised
friendship for the next ten years,
I would have been
able to keep it.*

74. Fade away

And maybe one day
you'll come back
to revisit this very moment
because after all this time
the memories
they'd never fade away.

75. Memories

Memories
how tragical and beautiful they are!
Honey filled jar
kept in sunlight,
mystic birds soaring
over the puddles of water
or even
the sound of a bell
ringing in distant
reminds me
of all the things
I have never witnessed.
Are those my memories,
or the fragments of
my imagination
that I've stored upon the years?

76. You weren't there

How could you forget
everything we had
in a blink of an eye?
All the nights we spent,
planning all of our wonderful pranks.
Lemons in the new shoes,
glues in their hats,
eggs in the balcony
and juice stains on their mats.
You had promised
that you'd save me
if anything went wrong,
but you weren't there
and you never took me along.
So tell me why
I'm still thinking of you?
Your pretty smiles
and witty replies,
still the fragrance of you
floating along my eyes.
Now it's been a long time
since we've even fought,

and I poke at you again and again
because atleast then we'd talked.
My sisters still ask about you,
and I know that you miss them too,
but how could they forget like you,
for they thought of you as a sibling new.

77. A hundred year old tree

I saw a tree today,
which was supposedly
a hundred years old.
My fingertips
grazed upon the skin
of the tree and
the realization hit my heart.
Someone, a hundred years ago,
planted a seed
that grew up to be this tree
or maybe the growing of this tree
was an accident.
But what a beautiful
accident it was!
The fingerprints of thousands
still embedded in the trunk,
the tears of the tragical romance
still stuck along the girth
and the memories
of the laughs

still floating around the bark.
How emollient was the idea
that I shared my moment
of peace and happiness
with the memories
of many others
and maybe, if I'm lucky,
someday, someone might
share their moment
with a memory of mine
flowed through the tree.

78. The friend I had is not you

We don't talk anymore
but I still think of you,
in the little things
that you taught me.
Your smiles
come up shouting
from the cycles
that we once rode together.
The laughs
scream at me
from the gardens
we spilled our hearts open in.
The hotels
that we always had our parties at,
still echoes
the shutter of our cameras.
The pavement still misses,
the long walks
and our everyday gossip.
Perhaps it was all right

that I can't call you anymore,
for the friend I had
is not you.

79. Lost time

It's ten years
from the day
That we first bumped into each other.
Eight years
since we became
the best duo of the town.
Five years
since we parted ways
to accomplish our goals.
Three years
since we've talked.
And gosh!
How much I missed
the sound of your laughs
each time I cracked
the lame puns I make.
It's not a sad idea
that I miss you.
It's sad that
it has been too long
from the first day
that you stumbled

in my life,
and I think
we lost too much
of the time we had
trying to look forward
and losing what we had
at that moment.

80. The epilogue

I want to write
a magical epilogue.
Two friends,
happily laughing together
eating cheap pizza
straight out of the box
while watching
a comedy movie of their choice.
I wish to write that.
I didn't have it.
I didn't even have an ending.
I wish
real life endings
atleast had an epilogue,
even if a sad one.

About The Poet

Ishita Akolkar, a budding engineer by the mind is also a poet by heart. Her journey as a poet started when she was 4, writing poetries in the name of homework. She has written various types of poetry: haikus, sonnets, couplets, free verse, and many more. At the age of 16, she wrote her first book 'The Unscrambled Heart'. Now being a student at an engineering college, she has started the first student-managed magazine 'The Concept', and is the director and the editor-in-chief. Started as a hobby, and now she writes to make people feel and heal. Having accomplished such great things, her journey as a poet has just started.

Previous Work By The Poet

"The Unscrambled Heart"

The book "The Unscambled Heart" is a collection of poetries by Ishita Akolkar, a young poetess. The poetries are a pure reflection of the poetess's heart. It is divided into five volumes, which reflect her thoughts on feminism, equalitarianism, and also winsomeness toward nature. I surely recommend all poetry lovers opt for this book. I really appreciate the presentable ways of her thoughts.

-Dr. Gulshan Avadia Ayachit,

Consultant Physiotherapist, MPT (SPORTS)

"The Unscrambled Heart" talks about love and literature in a way that is so nostalgic. Reading it feels like it gave you the detour around your childhood. It's a collection of feelings that we all have felt, put into beautifully coherent poetries. The writing style is lovely. Each piece of poetry is adorned with its interpretation of the world, the liberty of the reader to interpret it is marvelous.

-Twisha Patel,

Engineering student/Poet

www.ingramcontent.com/pod-product-compliance
Lightning Source LLC
Chambersburg PA
CBHW062219150726
47991CB00006B/2349